THE GOOD GOLF GUIDE

IMPROVE YOUR PUTTING

This material previously appeared in *Improve Your Golf*.
This volume compiled by Paul Foston and Sally Hiller.

CLB 3296
© Eaglemoss Publications Ltd 1989, 1990, 1991, 1992

This edition published in 1995 by SMITHMARK Publishers,
a division of U.S. Media Holdings, Inc.,
16 East 32nd Street, New York NY 10016

SMITHMARK books are available for bulk purchase for sales promotion and
premium use. For details write or call the manager of special sales,
SMITHMARK Publishers, Inc.
16 East 32nd Street, New York,
NY 10016; (212) 532-6600

Produced by CLB Publishing
Godalming Business Centre
Woolsack Way, Godalming, Surrey, UK

ISBN 0-8317-7479-7

Printed in Hong Kong
10 9 8 7 6 5 4 3 2 1

PICTURE CREDITS
Photographs: 9, Colorsport, 10, 18(b) Phil Sheldon
Photography, 25(b) Yours in Sport, 25(tl) Allsport/David
Cannon, 25(tr) Phil Sheldon Photography, 26 Allsport/David
Cannon, 30, 34 Golf Picture Library, 35 Phil Sheldon
Photography, 37 Yours in Sport, 47 Allsport/David Cannon,
49(b) Phil Sheldon Photography, 51(b) Allsport/David Cannon,
52 Colorsport, 54 Yours in Sport, 56 Phil Sheldon
Photography, 60(b) Allsport/David Cannon, 62(l) Charles
Briscoe-Knight, 67, 68(tr) Yours in Sport, 68(tl) Colorsport,
68(b), 69(t) Phil Sheldon Photography, 69(br) Allsport/
David Cannon
All other photographs: Eaglemoss/Phil Sheldon

Illustrations: Chris Perfect/ Egg Design

Cover: Centre: Allsport/David Cannon
Centre left: Yours in Sport
All others: Eaglemoss Publications

IMPROVE YOUR PUTTING

SMITHMARK

CONTENTS

INTRODUCTION

Drive for show and putt for dough – golfers everywhere, professional as well as amateur, will appreciate the truth of the saying. Putting is the make-or-break of any round of golf, and whilst its importance is universally acknowledged, it is this area of the game that so often gets the least attention. As you aim for perfection from tee to green, you must allow time to perfect your putting. A missed putt can cancel out the advantage of a 280-yard drive; miss four or five short putts in a round and you will wonder why you cannot play below your handicap. This book will help you to understand all there is to know about putting. It shows the variations in style, grip and technique while at the same time outlining the key points necessary to becoming a consistent putter.

Putting can be straightforward if the green is flat and true, but what about grain, cross-green slopes and putting up- or downhill? Green awareness is crucial if you are to hole putts with any degree of consistency. Finally, to become a proficient putter you must learn the basics and practise the correct techniques. The practice drills suggested in this book will help you develop your feel and touch, and in the process show you how to avoid those dreaded three-putts.

**Fuzzy Zoeller favours an open
putting address position. This
allows him to follow through on
the line of the putt more easily
than with a square set-up.**

IMPROVE YOUR TECHNIQUE

Very few people take putting lessons because they feel there isn't much they need to learn. How wrong they are! There are many different points to consider if you are to putt with consistency: your grip, stance, posture and stroke are but a few. Ben Crenshaw is recognised as a world-class putter, so we analyse his stroke.

An aggressive putter who hits the ball towards the back of the cup, Arnold Palmer has retained a strong putting technique over the years.

Putting

Almost half your shots in any round are putts so it is vital to develop a good stroke. If you putt well you are halfway to recording a decent score. Good putting is so important that just a handful of missed putts per round can mean the difference between a 19 and a 24 handicap.

The object of every putt is to hole the ball. If you don't, try to ensure that the ball is past the hole but near enough so that your next shot is from close range. Anything more than two putts per green is a waste of strokes.

After hitting tee and fairway shots 200yd (182m) or more, you finish every hole by putting the ball into the cup. Putts vary in distance from a 90ft (27m) one from the edge of a large green to a mere tap-in from the edge of the hole. However, most putts are between 2-30ft (0.5-9m).

Because a putt is normally quite short, it needs the shortest swing and least energy of any shot. Yet good putting requires precise stroke-making.

ROLLING THE BALL

Putting requires a unique technique – rolling the ball along the ground. It is the only shot where the ball does not travel through the air. The ball travels over a special surface – the green – and you use a specially designed club – the putter.

The putter has the least loft of any club – between 2° and 4° – so you cannot use it for gaining height on the ball. It is also the shortest club in the bag and the most up-right. It has a small club-head and is not built for distance.

Head start
You should keep your head still while you putt. You can practise this indoors, by resting your head against a wall while putting on a carpet. Stand close to the wall and touch it gently with your head. Keep your head there so it can't move as you putt along the side of the wall.

LEFT EYE OVER BALL

PUTT IT RIGHT

Although the putting stroke is the shortest of all, it is vital to get it right. Stand parallel to the line of the putt with your left eye directly over the ball. The clubhead travels along this same line for most of the stroke.

Your shoulders, hips and toes are parallel to the line of the putt.

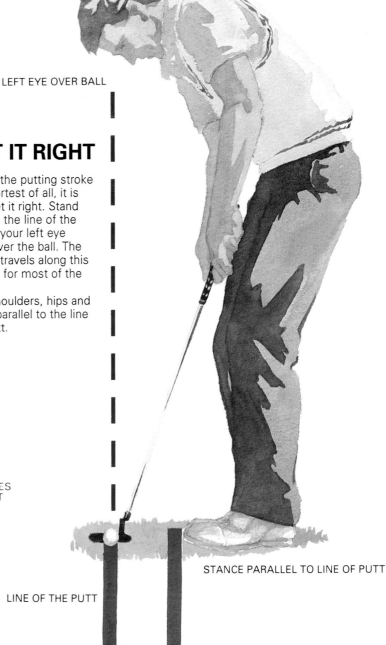

STANCE PARALLEL TO LINE OF PUTT

LINE OF THE PUTT

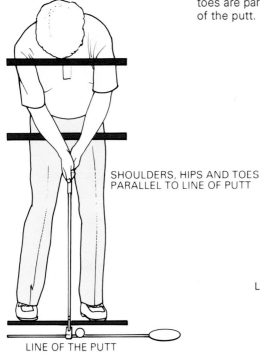

SHOULDERS, HIPS AND TOES PARALLEL TO LINE OF PUTT

LINE OF THE PUTT

GETTING TO GRIPS

1 PLACE LEFT HAND ON GRIP
Leaving a gap at the top, grip the club lightly with the middle, third and little fingers of your left hand. Point your forefinger down the shaft and hold your thumb above the flat front side.

2 ADD RIGHT HAND
Slide the little, third and middle fingers of your right hand against your middle left finger. Rest your left thumb against the centre of the shaft. Point both forefingers down the shaft.

3 COMPLETE THE GRIP
Wrap the forefinger of your right hand round the grip and rest your right thumb down the shaft. Let your left forefinger lie across your right hand. A straight line runs through wrist, hand and shaft.

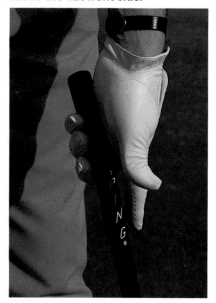
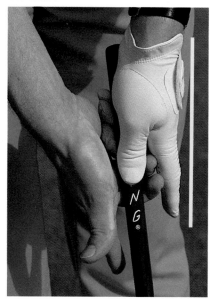
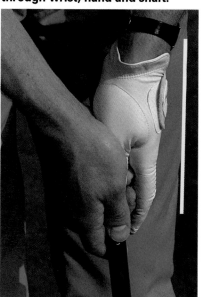

THE PUTTING STROKE

1 YOUR ADDRESS POSITION
The ball is opposite the inside of your left heel and your left eye is directly over the ball. Stand parallel to the line of the putt.

2 THE BACKSTROKE
Take the clubhead back straight. Your hands, arms and shoulders form one unit – a triangle which moves but never changes shape. Keep your head and lower body still.

pro tip

Feel the pendulum action
You can achieve the correct putting motion by practising the stroke with an object such as a short strip of wood trapped between your elbows. This makes your hands, arms and shoulders move as one and helps create an even pendulum action. Practise this until it feels natural.

LINE OF THE PUTT

Before you make your stroke you must decide on the line of the putt. This is not necessarily a straight line between ball and target – the ball-to-target line – because the roll of the ball will be affected by slopes.

To find the line of the putt try to visualize the path of your ball between its start position and the hole. If the green slopes from left down to right, the ball travels in the same direction, so compensate by selecting a point left of the hole at which to aim your putt. A straight line between the ball and this imaginary hole is called the line of the putt. A ball putted towards the imaginary hole curves with the slope and into the actual hole.

The exact point at which you aim depends on the severity of the slope and the length of the shot. The longer the putt and the greater the slope, the further away from the actual hole you should aim. This is because the more extreme conditions make the ball break further from the original line of the putt.

As well as assessing cross-slopes, you must take into account up and down slopes. An uphill putt needs a firmer strike than a down-hill stroke.

Much of visualization is common sense, but to be really good at it requires practice and experience. The more you putt, the easier you'll find it to judge the pace and direction.

AIM AND GRIP

Once you have established the line of the putt, aim the clubface square on to it. Some putters have a mark on the clubhead to help you aim correctly. Then you take up your grip.

There are almost as many putting grips as there are individual players but the reverse overlap is the most popular putting grip in today's game. It is similar to the standard overlap grip, with one difference: the forefinger of the left

3 THROUGH IMPACT
The throughstroke follows the same straight line as the backstroke. Keep your left wrist firm through impact to ensure the clubhead is pulled smoothly through the ball.

4 ENDING THE STROKE
The clubhead continues to the same height as the top of the backstroke. Your hands, arms and shoulders still move as one. Let your head rotate slightly to the left after impact.

hand changes places with the little finger of the right hand. This change helps to keep your left hand, arm and shoulder moving correctly through the ball.

POSTURE AND ALIGNMENT

The key point about putting posture is that you stand so that your eyes are directly over the ball at address. This gives you a clear view of the line of the putt and makes aiming easier. It usually means that you have to stand with your knees slightly bent and your back bent from the waist.

Because the putter is the shortest, most upright, club in the bag you stand close to the ball. With your feet about 12in (30cm) apart, stand so that the ball is opposite the inside of your left heel. By placing the ball forward in your stance you hit it on the upstroke. This produces topspin and gives a consistent roll. Your weight is evenly spread throughout.

As with all golf strokes, alignment is crucial. when putting you align your feet, knees, hips and shoulders parallel to line of putt.

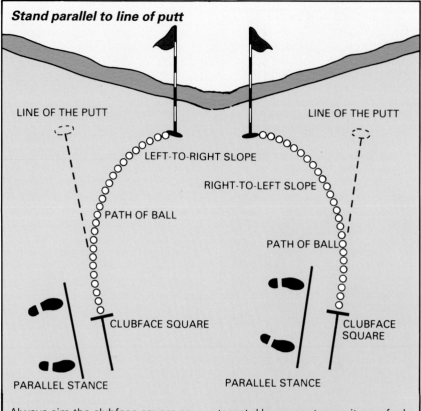

Stand parallel to line of putt

LINE OF THE PUTT

LINE OF THE PUTT

LEFT-TO-RIGHT SLOPE

RIGHT-TO-LEFT SLOPE

PATH OF BALL

PATH OF BALL

CLUBFACE SQUARE

CLUBFACE SQUARE

PARALLEL STANCE

PARALLEL STANCE

Always aim the clubface square on to the line of the putt and stand parallel to this line. Depending on the type and severity of the slope, this line may point left or right of the target. However strange it may feel to aim the clubface and align your body away from the target, it is the correct method – otherwise you hit a poor, badly aimed shot.

Judging pace and distance
To help you develop a feel for length, practise this simple routine. Place five balls in a line at 12in (30cm) intervals from the hole. Starting with the one nearest the hole, try to sink each ball in turn.

For each putt set yourself up carefully and assess the length of the stroke. Repeat until your back and throughstrokes are automatically the correct length to hole the ball.

THE STROKE

The putting stroke is dictated by your hands, arms and shoulders – which move as one unit. There is no body rotation, unlike full iron and wood shots. This is why it is vital to align your shoulders correctly at address.

Take the clubhead back with your hands, arms and shoulders moving together. The length of the backstroke is determined by the length of the putt. The clubhead travels in a straight line for most of the stroke, and only briefly moves inside the line of the putt as it nears the top of the backstroke.

Follow the same path into impact, keeping your left wrist firm. This allows the clubhead to be pulled through the ball on the correct line and prevents your right hand from flicking at it. Accelerate the clubhead through impact. Keep your head and lower body still, while allowing the clubhead to swing in a pendulum motion. The back and throughstrokes are of equal length.

Avoid green tension

Of all the strokes in golf, holing a putt just when you really need to gives you the greatest psychological lift. You know you can do it, but pressure has a nasty habit of undermining every golfer's technique at some time or other – no matter how good or confident the player happens to be.

If you can stay relaxed on the greens in a competition, your putting stroke remains with you all the way to the 18th hole of the match. Avoiding green tension is the key to putting well under pressure.

Cast your mind back to a couple of your best competition rounds – your putting was probably on song. On days like this – when the hole looks like a bucket – the putts

HOLING OUT UNDER PRESSURE
There are many ways to avoid tension on the greens – it's essential you have a system that works for you. If you can stay relaxed on the greens your putting is more likely to stand up to the most intense pressure. Whether it's a shortish putt on the 18th to secure a good score, or a curling left to righter to win a match, you can be confident of knocking it in.

STRAIGHT AND NARROW

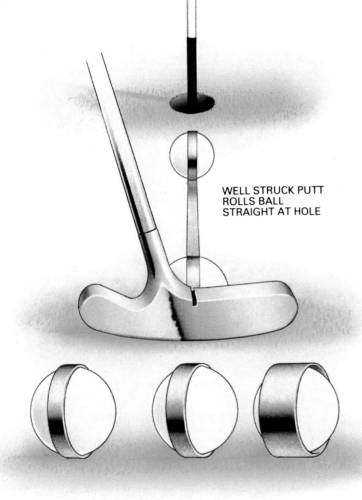

WELL STRUCK PUTT
ROLLS BALL
STRAIGHT AT HOLE

RAISED RIDGES VARY IN WIDTH
AROUND EACH BALL

The perfect putting stroke strikes the ball slightly on the up with the putter face square to the intended line – the result is a smooth roll on the ball.

A set of three golf balls is manufactured, each with a raised ridge around its circumference. The idea is to set each ball rolling dead straight without it toppling over to one side – achieve this and you know a putt is correctly struck.

Start practising with the ball that has the widest ridge – this is the easiest of the three and gives you some early confidence. As you become more proficient move on to the next ball with a narrower ridge. If you perform

this exercise successfully with the final ball, you can be confident that your putting stroke is in pretty good shape.

If you can't find these golf balls at a pro shop near you, paint a stripe around one of your practice balls. Take a putt with the stripe aiming straight at the hole. If it continues to point along the same line for its entire journey, you've struck the ball squarely and correctly.

Any sidespin – the ruin of every missed putt – is unmistakable as the stripe becomes more of a blur than a straight line.

SMOOTH STROKE

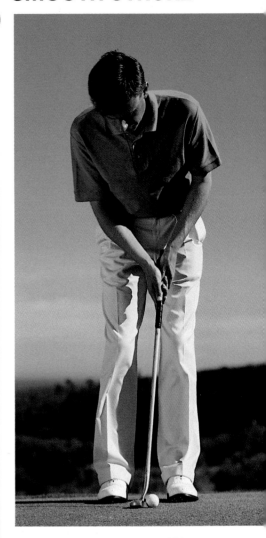

1 RELAXED OVER THE BALL
Staying relaxed at address is one of the keys to success over a long putt. Position the ball opposite your left heel – this helps you to stroke the ball slightly on the up to give it overspin. Your hands should be at least level with the ball – ahead is fine but behind is potentially disastrous.

pro tip

Shake to relax
Making sure your muscles are free from tension is essential when you're on the green. Relaxation promotes feel and touch – two vital qualities to good putting. If you struggle to achieve this, a simple exercise might solve the problem.

Before you address the ball, rest your putter against your leg and allow your arms to hang down freely. Loosely shake your hands a couple of times to relieve any muscle tightness – when it comes to standing over the ball you should be nicely relaxed.

2 SMOOTHLY BACK
Maintaining a light grip, sweep the putter back low away from the ball. Make sure the triangle formed by your shoulders and arms remains the same as at address. For a putt of this length try to keep your wrists firm. If you allow them to hinge it's easy to lose control of the putter head – this upsets the angle of the clubface at a critical moment during the stroke.

3 DOWN AND THROUGH
Accelerate the putter smoothly into impact – the ball position at address ensures the clubhead travels up and generates overspin to set the ball rolling. If you hit down on a putt the ball usually hops into the air making it extremely difficult to judge pace. Keep your left wrist firm to ensure your hands are in front of the putter head for as long as possible.

tend to drop at crucial stages in the round. This is the difference between a potentially winning score and an average one.

Because you have to be more precise on the greens than elsewhere on the course, tension is disastrous. It destroys the most important ingredient of any putting stroke – feel.

Your putter starts to behave erratically as you struggle to control the line and length of even the simplest of putts. You're in for a frustrating time as the ball keeps slipping past the hole.

TENSION TRIGGERS

There are several causes of ten-sion on the greens. On a **good round** in a competition there are many pressures on you to keep your score intact. Probably the greatest of these is remaining solid when it comes to the business of holing out.

When your **confidence is low** it's easy to imagine the hole is almost shrinking before your eyes – knocking in a putt of any real distance can seem like the hardest task in the world.

This doubt often stems from missing a short putt or two early in the round – your confidence has taken a battering.

The golfing muscles can also tighten at the prospect of a **difficult putt**. Every golfer has a tension trigger – the one that breaks from left to right is the most commonly disliked.

Perhaps you find that putts from one particular range are the stuff that nightmares are made of. And a downhill putt on a slippery green is a real test of nerve, even for the professionals.

Whatever green experience triggers tension for you, don't be reconciled to disaster. Rather than expecting the worst, set out to break your run of missed putts.

Even if you've never felt the slightest bit nervous over a putt – which is unlikely – certain techniques promote a reliable putting stroke when it really matters. Striking your putt within a well rehearsed groove makes all the difference.

The hands play a vital role in the putting stroke, so first examine your grip. Do you feel in control of the clubhead? There's no right or wrong way to hold a putter – styles depend on individual taste and preference.

If you're a wristy putter – rather in the style of Gary Player – always grip the club lightly in both hands. The same applies if – like Tom Watson for instance – you're a shoulders and arms putter. Never grip the club too tightly – it restricts your feel for the clubhead, making assessment of weight tricky.

GRIP PRESSURE

Check your grip pressure is the same throughout the stroke. A consistently light grip helps you to make a smooth stroke and accurately judge the weight of a putt – it also reduces the risk of the putter face opening or closing.

To achieve success on the greens you need a sound putting stroke. Though you can copy certain fundamentals from the professionals, there should always be a personal touch to your putting if you're to be comfortable.

Only if a style is your own can you feel truly comfortable over the ball. A natural stance is a real tension beater – if there's a key to holing more putts, this is it. Sticking rigidly to one particular technique can hold back your putting.

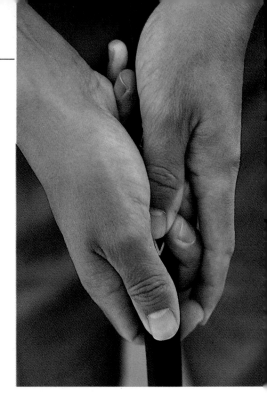

PALMS FACING
You have the perfect putting grip when both hands work in harmony throughout the stroke. The reverse overlap – the most commonly used putting grip – is one of the best ways to achieve this. Both thumbs point straight down the shaft with the palms facing each other. A constant grip pressure encourages the hands to operate as one unit.

Making a good stroke
In the winter months greens are naturally more bumpy than in hot sunny conditions. The grass tends to be a bit woolly which prevents the ball from rolling smoothly. You're bound to see the occasional good putt wander off line on an uneven surface.

In these conditions concentrate on making a good stroke at the ball and don't worry too much if the putts don't drop. It's easy to start doubting your putting stroke – thinking there's something wrong with you when often it's the greens that are at fault. Try to be patient and avoid changing your technique or your putter – good greens are usually just round the corner.

Stroke of genius
Major championships are the ultimate test of nerve for professionals – some cope and others crumble. Few golfers experience such pressures, but you can learn a valuable lesson just by watching.

When Seve Ballesteros strode on to the final green in the 1984 Open at St Andrews, he knew if he holed the 12ft (4m) putt the title was his.

Because Seve's putting style is his own he is able to feel comfortable over the ball. Even under intense pressure his stance is relaxed and his grip free from tension. A smooth, unhurried stroke saw the ball drop in the right edge of the hole – the claret jug was his for the second time.

When you're faced with an important putt, take time to compose yourself. Make a couple of practice strokes to give you a feel for the distance and, most importantly, to relax your muscles. Few experiences in golf are more satisfying than holing a putt when it matters.

Perfect your putting

It's the most talked and written about aspect of golf, and it's often the most frustrating. None of this is pure coincidence – putting is the most crucial area in any round of golf.

A look at the 1990 European Tour statistics is proof in itself. Bernhard Langer averaged less than 29 putts per round having played in 17 tournaments and finished fourth in the Order of Merit with prize money of over £420,000.

The putting stroke requires less movement than any other shot – yet a sound technique on the greens eludes golfers the world over. Lack of ability is rarely to blame – not enough practice is often the culprit.

There are endless opportunities to practise your putting. You don't need much space and you can putt indoors as well as outdoors – even if it's only putting to a chair leg.

Whether it's on the carpet or on

STATISTICAL EVIDENCE
When you're next in a competition at your home club, talk to a golfer with a good score – he's likely to be someone who putted well. When that happens, every long putt tends to finish close and the short ones drop with monotonous regularity. It's seldom down to luck – hard work on the practice putting green is usually the only way to achieve this type of success.

A FEEL FOR DISTANCE

1 COMFORTABLE ADDRESS
Above all you must feel comfortable and relaxed at address on the greens. Think of grip pressure – it must remain consistent throughout the stroke. Check the alignment of the putter head – it should be square to the line you want the ball to roll along.

2 INSIDE TAKEAWAY
On a longish putt, sweep the putter back slightly inside the ball-to-target line. The distance you are from the hole determines the length of your backswing. Whatever style of putting stroke you adopt, there should be no movement from the waist down.

pro tip

Trial and error

Every golfer loses confidence on the greens from time to time – it usually only needs a couple of putts to drop for your state of mind to be transformed. But sometimes it pays to search for an alternative cure.

Most club professionals are happy to let you on to the practice green with a variety of putters. The face is usually taped up for protection, but you soon develop an overall feel for the club.

Take about half a dozen balls and stroke putts across the green swapping different clubs. It doesn't take long to discover which of the putters you like and which are totally unsuitable.

More often than not, practising with a variety of putters makes you realize that the old faithful you were about to dispense with is not quite as bad as you thought. Either way, you stand an excellent chance of restoring lost confidence.

3 RETURN TO SQUARE
With a fundamentally sound putting stroke the position at impact mirrors that at address. The putter face returns square to the ball with the hands leading the clubhead through impact. Strike the ball slightly on the up to generate the necessary overspin.

4 SET THE PACE
Smoothly accelerate the putter head through impact – it should travel slightly inside the line again to complete the in-to-in path of the clubhead. Only now should you look up. Repeat the same putt several times to test your ability to judge pace consistently.

the putting green, there's just one factor that should remain the same – always introduce variety into your practice to ensure your interest level remains high.

FREEDOM OF CHOICE

There's no right or wrong way to putt – it's very much a case of finding a system that works for you. Nick Faldo is a shoulders and arms putter. Gary Player has a wristy, stabbing type putting stroke. The only similarity is that their techniques are awesomely effective.

There are certain fundamentals which are consistent with most great putters – hands directly above the ball at address; a constant grip pressure throughout the stroke and the putter blade square to the intended line.

Once you have a comfortable style based on sound technique, the next step is to build into your game a method that works over and over again even under severe pressure. The practice putting green is the place to groove a repeatable stroke.

Place several balls in a circle around a hole to sharpen your short range putts. Attempt to knock in each ball and only move on to another drill when each one is in the hole. If you miss one, start all over again – this adds an exciting element of pressure into the exercise.

To improve your feel for distance, stroke a ball from one side of the putting green to the other. Then attempt to stop another dozen balls on precisely the same spot – the tighter the grouping

the better your judgment of line and weight.

COMPETITIVE EDGE

It's always a good idea to set aside a few minutes for pre-round preparation, particularly if you're in a competition.

An excellent way to brush up on your stroke is to hit several long putts. Concentrate on making a smooth swing – note how the ball comes off the putter face. You should be looking to sharpen your judgment of distance.

It's seldom advisable to practise short putts just before a competitive round. It only needs a couple to slip by the hole and your confidence takes a dive. This is unlikely to have you stepping on to the 1st green in a very positive frame of mind.

Always use the same ball on the practice putting green as you would on the course. Don't carelessly pluck a two piece solid ball from your bag if you intend playing a balata out on the course. The difference in feel between the two is enormous.

COPY SLAMMIN' SAM

As soon as you walk on to the 1st green, take a close look at the length and texture of the grass. It may differ slightly from the type found on the practice green and have an effect on the roll of your ball.

If you find you're having a bad day on the greens – and it happens to everyone from time to time – try adopting the Sam Snead philosophy. He was once quoted as saying about short putts, 'if you're going to miss one, miss it quick'. You may be pleasantly surprised – a carefree approach might make the putts start to drop again.

Blind spot
Putting is such a precision art that it's easy to tie yourself up in knots over technique. Do you crouch over the ball or stand upright? Is an open or square stance best? How do you grip the club? The permutations are seemingly endless.

Sometimes it's a good idea to forget about the text book and rely solely on feel. Putting with your eyes closed can help you achieve this – it relieves tension in your body and places the emphasis on your stroke.

Address the ball with your eyes open. When you feel comfortable, close your eyes and putt the ball towards the hole. Before you open them again, try to predict where the ball has finished – short or long, pulled left, pushed right or dead straight.This exercise increases your control over the putter head and develops your feel for line and length on the greens.

Listen – don't look
One of the keys to Nick Faldo's 1990 Open victory at St Andrews was his impeccable holing out. His only 3 putt of the entire championship was from long range at the treacherous Road hole. That was in the final round and by then the tournament was his.

Copying a technique practised by Nick Faldo may help you to hole out more regularly – but it's something you need to experiment with on the practice putting green before you carry it out in a competition.

On short putts wait for the sound of the ball dropping into the hole before you look up. This encourages you to concentrate on the stroke rather than ball direction.

Looking up before striking the ball causes miss-hits and is one of the major causes of missing short putts.

Crenshaw: master putter

The gentle Texan Ben Crenshaw is acknowledged by his fellow professionals and golfing experts as the best putter in the world. He studied the technique of Bobby Jones to help develop his near perfect stroke. Crenshaw's touch is legendary – he putts well on even the most difficult greens.

Believing putting to be an art not a science, Ben relies on simple fundamentals – he never allows himself to get bogged down in the more remote complexities of technique. The result is a pure and natural stroke.

PUTT PRIORITIES

The 1984 Masters champion recommends a putting style that suits the individual but is based on correct principles – a comfortable grip that keeps the blade square, a smooth arm swing and good feel.

You need to combine sound basic technique with an ability to read the greens. Ben accepts that speed determines the line when gauging a putt, and poorly judged speed rather than line is the cause of most three putts.

TEXAN TALENT
Ben Crenshaw combines a natural talent for judging slope and pace with superb technique, and is one of the game's finest putters. Both his long approach putts and touch around the hole are masterly.

Controlled comfort
Crenshaw holds the putter with a light and perfectly balanced grip. Both thumbs point down the shaft, leaving his hands square to the target line. His wrists stay firm throughout the stroke.

He believes every golfer should find a comfortable grip – one that works for the individual, rather than following a style that suits someone else. But try out the Texan's method, adapting it to your own game, if you're struggling to hole putts.

BOTH
THUMBS
DOWN
SHAFT

Trust your first instincts when reading greens is Crenshaw's advice. On long putts, worry about the weight of the shot more than the line – a putt that's the right distance is never far away. He treats short putts as 70% line and 30% feel. Keeping his head down until he hears the putt drop, he thinks about the stroke rather than the hole.

SMOOTH TEMPO

You can learn a lot from watching Crenshaw. He uses an arm rather than a wristy stroke. This makes his striking consistent – you must have perfect timing to putt well with a wrist stroke. Ben's action is smooth and the tempo is constant throughout the swing.

The Texan's grip is conventional – a reverse overlap. He points his thumbs down the shaft, ensuring that his hands are square to the target, and keeps the putter blade square throughout the stroke.

Like many top pros, he positions the ball opposite his left heel to promote a good roll. Although Crenshaw plays with a perfect pendulum stroke, his stance is slightly less standard.

Most top golfers position the ball so that their eyes are directly over it. But Ben putts with the ball further away from his body. He feels that this gives him the freedom to swing his arms rhythmically with no restrictions.

PUTTING LANE

When Ben visualizes a putt he doesn't just imagine a line, he sees a lane the width of the hole. This makes him feel more confident – he knows if he sets the ball off down the lane with the proper speed it has a chance of going in.

If you're struggling with your putting, go back to the basics. Even Crenshaw loses his surgeon's precision now and again, but he persists with the simple techniques he's always used. Don't despair if your putts aren't dropping – if they keep coming close they'll eventually go in.

Ben hasn't become the putter he is by just playing – he's worked for hours on the practice putting green to perfect his stroke. Follow his example – work out a practice routine involving both easy and difficult long and short putts.

PROVEN PUTTING STYLE

Use the basics but don't be afraid to experiment is Crenshaw's advice. The Ryder Cup player adopts a near standard technique on the greens. The only part of his set-up that is slightly unconventional is his ball position. Although he places the ball opposite his left heel – as many top golfers do to promote good roll – he plays it well away from his body.

Most golf teachers say that your eyes should be directly over the ball at address so that you can see the line easily. But Ben's method is effective, giving his arms the freedom to swing in a relaxed way. Crenshaw provides evidence that sound basics and an individual style are a powerful combination.

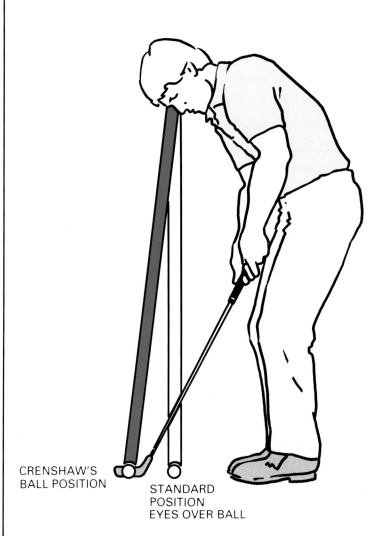

CRENSHAW'S BALL POSITION

STANDARD POSITION EYES OVER BALL

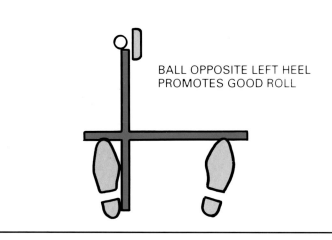

BALL OPPOSITE LEFT HEEL PROMOTES GOOD ROLL

Far left: David Graham acknowledges the Augusta galleries. Apart from his US Open and USPGA wins, he has six victories on the US Tour dating back to 1972.

Left: Plumb-bobbing on the greens brought success for Graham, always a reliable putter. Consistently high finishes on the US Tour won him career earnings well in excess of $2 million.

Below: When he exploded on the European golfing scene in 1986, many people compared José-Maria Olazabal to his more famous fellow Spaniard Severiano Ballesteros. However, Olazabal's performances ever since have confirmed him as a great player in his own right.

HOW TO BEAT THE YIPS

There is nothing worse than three-putting a green. It is such a waste because it usually means that you have missed a three- or four-foot putt. These short putts are normally missed because of tension in your grip, which in most cases leads to a jerky stroke. Should this happen regularly you can only have what is commonly described as the 'yips'. We take a look at two players – Sam Torrance and Bernhard Langer – to see how they combated this dreadful disease.

Craig Stadler holds his hand to his head after just missing a short putt that would have kept the US in the lead at the 1985 Ryder Cup. The European team took the cup the following day.

How to beat the yips

No golfer with a heart would subject someone to a bout of the yips – not even their own worst enemy. Sufferers go through periods of sheer hell as one putt after another fails even to threaten the hole.

For those who have never been through the yips, it's a problem that's difficult to understand. The right hand tends to take over and jerk the putter head into the back of the ball. It seems like the club has a will of its own.

No matter how hard you try to stay in control of your stroke, the ball still shoots off in all directions. It can get to the stage where every short putt is a potential twitch just waiting to happen. And the faster the greens the more frightening it becomes.

ADDED PRESSURE

If you're unfortunate enough to suffer from the yips, missing three-footers is not your only problem. Poor putting also places enormous pressure on the rest of your game.

You start to believe that almost no putt is holeable. The more approach shots you hit, the more you feel you have to knock the ball stone dead to stand any chance of making a birdie. Finishing on the green – but a long way from the hole – is almost worse than missing the target altogether. As you walk towards the green all you can think of is three putts.

It's easy to see why players with the yips seriously consider giving up golf – it gradually eats away at their entire game. However, the problem can be cured – Sam Torrance and Bernhard Langer are proof of that.

And beating the yips doesn't necessarily mean carrying a broom-handle putter for the rest of your golfing days, although it works for some people. Nor do you have to call on the services of the nearest hypnotist or sports psychologist.

More conventional remedies can be found, but it's important to understand that the yips don't

ANOTHER ONE SLIPS BY
Anyone who plays golf can sympathize with a player who regularly misses short putts. An affliction known as the yips, there's no worse feeling in golf, because it's difficult to know what went wrong. All you're left with is a sense of frustration and complete disbelief that you've missed from such close range. The problem is caused by both hands fighting against each other – once you get them to work in harmony you have a reliable system for holing out.

Hit and miss

Many golfers who suffer on the greens tend to miss putts in a fairly random manner. Left, right, short or long – on a bad day you might hit every one of these in close succession.

This is probably where putting differs most from any other part of your game. Every golfer hits one type of bad shot more than any other – a slice for instance. This makes it easy to spot the mistake when it happens and you can then work at correcting it. However, with putting, it's hard to identify where you're going wrong because putts tend to miss on different sides of the hole.

This is why your putting technique should be a style of your own – not some mechanical creation that you don't understand, adopted when cracks appear. Try to develop a stroke based on a combination of feel, individuality and five important qualities that are present in most successful styles:

● Eyes directly over the ball;
● Putter face square to the intended line;
● A light hold on the putter with equal grip pressure applied by both hands;
● A comfortable address position;
● A repetitive stroke.

Look at these areas when you're trying to identify a fault in your putting. Never rule out a change of putter either. This is by no means the best cure – your equipment is seldom to blame for bad putting. But a change often uncovers a lack of confidence – this may be the problem rather than any serious technical flaw.

disappear overnight. It takes time and you may have to experiment a little to find the system that works for you.

BACK TO SQUARE ONE

First, you need to go back to basics and look at what makes a good putting stroke. Two factors are common among great putters – a consistent angle between the left wrist and the shaft of the putter through impact, combined with a light, sensitive grip.

If you suffer from the yips, there's every chance that you're failing to perform one, or both, of these moves. So how do you go about building them into your putting stroke?

One of the most popular methods is a cross-handed putting grip. The main benefit of this technique is that it makes it easy to keep your left wrist firm throughout the stroke. It's very difficult to yip a putt if this move is part of your technique.

Another advantage of the cross-handed method is that it naturally pushes the back of your left hand through towards the hole. This keeps the putter face square and prevents the right hand taking over. These are two major steps towards eliminating a jerky putting stroke.

This is particularly important on the short putts, because once you're lined up correctly, you simply need a method that returns the putter face perfectly square to the ball at impact.

However, as you move further away from the hole, a square putter face isn't all you need. Good judgment of pace is just as important, because if you get the correct weight on a long putt, you're seldom too far away.

HOW FAR BACK?

While the yips usually refers to a stabbing movement into the ball, it's worth taking a look at the length of your backswing – particularly if you're struggling to find the correct length on many of your putts.

Bear in mind that the length of your backswing should determine the length of the putt. This allows you to accelerate the putter head smoothly into the back of the ball – the complete opposite of yipping

BAD CASE OF THE YIPS

1 GREAT EXPECTATIONS
The closer to the hole the more a golfer is prone to the yips. This is probably caused by expecting to hole short putts – worse still, so does everyone else – but no one presumes you should roll in one long putt after another. This poor state of mind often creates tension at address, particularly in your hands. As soon as this happens you're in danger of hitting a wide selection of very bad putts.

2 START OF YOUR PROBLEMS
This is a good example of one problem leading to another – if you're not relaxed at address it's extremely difficult to make a smooth backswing. It's more likely that you jerk the club back too quickly – at that precise moment you lose control of your putting stroke.

3 OUT OF CONTROL
A sure sign of the yips is the ball shooting off to the left the moment it leaves the putter face. This is caused by the right hand taking charge, which causes a hit rather than a stroke. Make sure you accelerate the putter head smoothly through impact – the ball merely gets in the way of your putting stroke.

4 MISSED AGAIN
This is a familiar – and extremely depressing – sight for any golfer stricken by the yips. The ball travels well left of the hole and often at speed. You should really aim to keep body movement to a minimum when you're over a putt – your shoulders, hands and arms are well capable of holding together your putting stroke.

a putt.

If your backswing is too short, you struggle to generate enough clubhead speed on the through-swing – you simply don't have time. This means you can forget about smooth acceleration into the back of the ball – you probably jerk the putter forward.

If you have too long a backswing you create a different set of problems. It's not a yip, but it leads to poor judgment of distance – and missed putts – because you decelerate the putter into impact. This is no less depressing than any other yipped putt.

pro tip

Hover for a smooth start
The yips aren't confined only to the throughswing – often the problem stems from not taking the putter back smoothly. If you jerk the putter away from the ball it's impossible to control line or length – no matter how near you are to the hole.

This annoying fault is often caused by pressing the putter too hard into the ground behind the ball. It's easy to drift into this bad habit, particularly if you're going through a crisis on the greens. Try a simple exercise – preferably in practice first – to help you cure this fault.

When you address the ball, hover the putter head just off the ground. This means the putter hangs more naturally – almost like a pendulum – and encourages you to start the backswing smoothly. It also helps you strike your putts on the up, which generates overspin and sets the ball rolling smoothly.

BEFORE AND AFTER
Bernhard Langer's putting problems are a legacy of his early golfing days in Germany. Slow greens – often in less than perfect condition – trained Langer to hit putts firmly at the back of the hole. He developed a truly magical touch and became a very good putter, particularly from close range. Even if the putts didn't drop he could blame the poor surface and not his stroke – Langer never suffered from a lack of confidence with his putting.

Moving on to the faster greens of the European and American Tours, Langer's orthodox putting stroke began to break down. Finding it hard to adjust to a change in pace, his backswing remained far too long, almost as though he were still playing on slow greens. To compensate, Langer decelerated the putter into the ball to prevent him hitting his putts too strongly. This is when the yips began to set in.

Every time Langer is plagued by the yips he finds a cure – such as the cross-handed putting grip. It's unorthodox and it doesn't look pretty – but it works because his left wrist doesn't break down through impact. It also takes the right hand out of the stroke.

This is why you need to experiment a little if you're going through major putting problems. Finding a system that works is all that matters – not how it looks.

Torrance beats the yips

When Sam Torrance held his arms aloft as he rolled in the winning putt of the 1985 Ryder Cup at The Belfry, few imagined that within three years his confidence on the greens would be completely destroyed by the dreaded yips.

The yips is the name given to the involuntary and disconcerting convulsion of the muscles in the hands and arms while trying to hole putts. The golfer jerks the ball way past the hole.

Many famous golfers have been affected by the yips over the years, and some of them have never fully recovered. Peter Alliss and Ben

Hogan both retired from playing because of their inability to hole out on the greens.

Bernhard Langer also suffered from the yips. While he has done well to regain some of his form, he is far from the putter he was when he won the Masters in 1985.

But while Langer's putting has never been his main strength,

Torrance was considered to have one of the smoothest strokes on the tour. When the yips came, his silky stroke was replaced by a jittery jab. He began to miss cuts and plummeted down the money list.

After a good 1987, when he finished ninth on the order of merit, he was hit by the yips and he

THE NEW SAM
The Scottish Ryder Cup star has turned to using a revolutionary new putter to combat the yips, which affected his performances in 1988. At 48in (120cm) the broom handle putter is considerably longer than any other on the market. This means Torrance can keep it steady with his chin throughout the stroke.

TORRANCE'S METHOD

1 THE ADDRESS POSITION

Sam aims the putter as normal. While gently holding the top of the putter with his left hand, he places the butt of the shaft under his chin. His right arm hangs relaxed down beside the shaft. He then places his right hand on a grip lower down the shaft. He lightly grips with his thumb and index finger, while his forefinger points down along the grip.

2 THE TAKEAWAY

With the left hand and the chin stabilizing the putter, Sam makes a slow deliberate backswing controlled by the right hand. His head and body remain perfectly still, while his eyes are directly over the ball. There is no sign of a loop, often a cause of missed putts.

3 THE STROKE

Sam accelerates through the ball with a smooth yet firm stroke as any good putter should do. The right hand guides the club, and also adds the force to the shot. But notice how lightly he holds the shaft with just his thumb and forefinger, giving him more feel and control. Throughout the whole movement Sam's head and body are quite still.

4 THE FOLLOWTHROUGH

His putter head swings through on a straight line towards the target. Sam's followthrough is the same length as his backswing, whatever the distance of the putt. His visor position shows that his head remains in exactly the same place throughout. He looks up only when the ball has gone.

slumped to 51st in 1988. Tension and nerves were to blame.

BROOM HANDLE

Sam is a fighter and he doesn't give up. After trying all the accepted ways of curing the ailment, he searched for a club that he could keep steady at all times. This led to the invention of the broom handle putter.

The putter has been a huge success for Torrance. His results improved dramatically. 1989 saw Sam regain his Ryder Cup place, and a very creditable 11th position on the money list.

Australian Peter Senior also benefited from this style of putter. He rests the butt of the shaft on his chest instead of his chin. He used it to win three events in quick succession in 1989 after having problems on the greens.

There has been some doubt about the legality of the putter. But the R and A, who control which clubs can be played, have given Sam's brainchild the all clear. And to avoid getting an unfair advantage, the players on the European Tour have agreed not to use the putter to gain relief when dropping the ball.

So Sam's invention seems destined to become one of the best ways to cure the most feared affliction in golf.

▲ CROSS HANDED
Sam tried all the accepted methods of curing the yips. He turned to using the cross handed grip, still favoured by Bernhard Langer. This style has helped the German regain his form, but it did not solve Sam's problems.

◄ CONVENTIONAL STYLE
For many years Sam putted conventionally, and was very successful. He was regarded as one of the finest putters on the tour, by both his fellow professionals and the public. His skill on the greens helped him to win many big tournaments – until he became afflicted by the convulsive jerky stroke known as the yips.

Try it for yourself
If you have problems with jerky putting, it may be worth your while trying a broom handle putter to steady your stroke. In price, these putters rank alongside the top of the range, so ask your local PGA professional if you can borrow a trial club. See whether it helps you to hole more putts before you go to the expense of buying one. The yips affect golfers in different ways – one player's cure may not work for everybody.

DIFFERENT TYPES OF PUTT

To be able to deal with all the varieties of putt that you are likely to encounter you will need to assess the green and its slopes. Visualisation, therefore, is a skill that you will need to acquire. Because all greens are different, speed must be carefully judged if you are to get close to the hole from long range. This section deals with the numerous putting situations that you are likely to encounter.

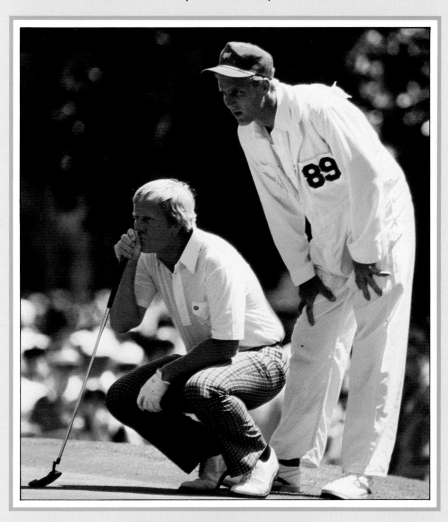

Winning the US Masters in 1986, at the age of 46, was all the more satisfying as Nicklaus' son, Jackie, was carrying his bag.

Putting from off the green

A putt from off the green is probably the only shot in golf which pride prevents golfers from playing. Many players reach for a lofted club anywhere near the green. But if you think putting from off the green is a stroke only for beginners, you're making a big mistake.

Try telling Jack Nicklaus that it's a shot for novices. In his famous head to head with Tom Watson in the final round of the 1977 Open Championship, Watson rolled in an outrageous putt from off the 15th green. Many would have chipped, but Watson knew that a putt was perfect for coaxing his ball over the bone-hard Turnberry terrain. The shot proved to be a crucial turning point – he went on to beat the Golden Bear.

The beauty of putting from off the green is that it's very straightforward. There's no need to play a delicate chip with your sand wedge – a shot that can so easily go wrong, particularly if your confi-

TAILORED TO YOUR NEEDS
Before you consider putting from off the green, you have to be certain that the ground conditions are just right. When they are, it's a tidy stroke that can help you get up and down with the minimum fuss. First, check the grass is closely mown so that your ball can roll smoothly all the way on to the putting surface. Then read the borrow – taking into account slopes before the green and on it. Pick out a precise line, set your sights and keep the stroke smooth.

dence isn't sky high.

The technique for putting off the green involves more of a shoulders and arms stroke. In comparison to your normal putting style you should keep wrist movement to a minimum. Also make sure you grip lightly with both hands to help improve your feel for distance.

In the right conditions it's a deadly stroke and shouldn't frighten you in the least. So, when do you reach for your putter rather than one of your irons?

CLEAR RUNWAY

Putt from off the green if the grass between you and the putting surface is fairly closely mown. It doesn't really matter if there are humps, hollows and slopes along the way. As long as your ball runs over them quite smoothly, you can judge the pace on the ball – if the grass is too long, you can't possibly get the weight right.

Walk up to the edge of the green looking out for divots or any other obstructions which might get in the way of your ball. Don't just putt round them.

Be even more wary of a sprinkler head on your line. If your ball comes into contact with one of these it could shoot off at almost any angle. Chip if you're in any doubt about whether you can avoid these pop-up problems.

If your ball is on a tight lie, with

Stick in the mud
Putting from off the green is generally not a good idea in winter. All the conditions are against you – soggy ground under foot, damp lush grass, maybe even surface water which can be difficult to spot.

All these factors drag your ball to a premature halt – you may need to hit the ball so hard to allow for this that it becomes almost impossible to judge speed accurately. You're likely to struggle to get down in 2.

In extremely wet conditions there's always a better option than putting from off the green. A chip and run with a mid iron is probably the best of the bunch. It gives you enough loft to avoid any wet areas – and generates very little backspin, which encourages your ball to roll.

Leading edge
Some putters are better suited than others if you're considering playing the toe-poke shot from the edge of the fringe. It all comes down to whether your putter has the properly shaped head.

The putter used by Mike Donald in the 1990 US Open at Medinah is just about perfect for this delicate shot. The toe is fairly square, so there's less chance of the ball squirting off at a strange angle.

This is a good basis for your decision. If the toe of your putter is quite square, or the edges are well defined, you should have no major problems striking the ball correctly and accurately.

If the head of your putter is a more rounded shape, don't even consider playing this shot. It's almost impossible to stroke the ball consistently in the direction you want – instead it flies off at any angle from the curved edges.

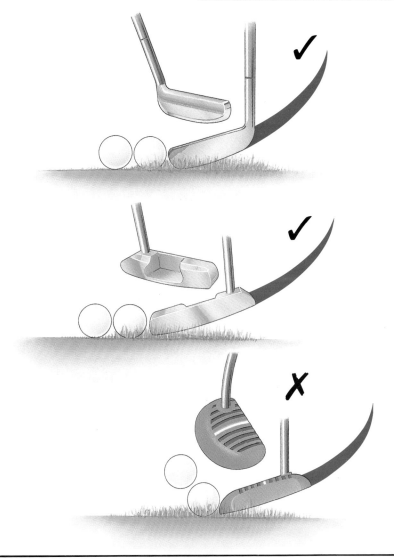

PUTTING FROM THE FRINGE

1 EASE THE PRESSURE

Many golfers find it difficult to play a chip shot when they're very close to the flag, mainly because you need an extremely delicate touch. This is when putting from fringe rough is a useful shot to have in your bag, particularly under pressure when you may be feeling a bit jumpy. However, you must be able to see the ball clearly. If the lie is any worse, don't attempt to use your putter.

2 KEEP IT SIMPLE

One of the great advantages of playing this shot is that you use a very simple technique based on your normal putting stroke. Position the ball centrally in your stance – this helps you to strike down more than you do with a putt from on the green.

3 DISTANCE GAUGE

The length of your backswing depends on two important factors – the distance you are from the hole and the thickness of the fringe grass. Experiment with this in practice – through a process of trial and error you can play the shot during a round without nagging doubts concerning technique hanging over you.

4 FIRM THROUGH THE BALL

Notice how there is no sign of the left wrist breaking down – the angle you set at address remains the same through impact. Also make sure the back of your left hand faces the target until completion of the throughswing – this helps push the putter face square through towards the hole.

very little grass around it, a putt from off the green can be a sensible shot. You often come across these lies when the ground is baked hard – when you do, it can come as something of a relief to be able to take out your putter.

From a tight lie, striking the ball correctly with your putter is easier than trying to nip the ball cleanly with a lofted iron. This is true provided there's no great distance to cover. As a rule, anywhere under 40yd (36m) and you should be safe taking out your putter – any further and the benefits of putting from off the green start to diminish with every step back you take.

In fact, this shot starts to become quite dangerous from extremely long range. Most golfers find that it's easy to miss-hit a shot completely when making an incredibly long backswing with a putter. Once you're beyond a certain point, a comfortable chip with a 7 iron is a more reliable system.

Creative putting

When your ball rests up against the fringe around the green, you can't place the clubhead behind the ball in the normal way. This in itself makes you feel uneasy and triggers doubts in your mind. It's also hard to deliver a good strike on the ball – grass is almost certain to deaden the blow.

These are the situations when you need to be creative. Try turning round your putter so that the toe points towards the hole (**1**). You find that the putter head sits closer to the middle of the ball, therefore boosting your chances of making a clean strike. This is difficult to achieve when the blade is at its normal angle.

Position the ball further back in your stance than normal. Other than that, don't introduce any major changes to your technique. Make a normal length backswing (**2**) and accelerate the putter head into the back of the ball. You may find the ball pops up in the air just after impact (**3**), but after that it should roll like a normal putt.

Every golfer knows how easy it is to make mistakes if you chip from this position, particularly under pressure. You can send your ball skimming through the green or make such feeble contact that you fail to move it at all. While striking with the toe of the putter may not be the easiest option, you at least get the ball moving forward at roughly the correct speed.

Long putts

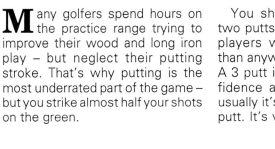

Many golfers spend hours on the practice range trying to improve their wood and long iron play – but neglect their putting stroke. That's why putting is the most underrated part of the game – but you strike almost half your shots on the green.

You shouldn't take more than two putts on any green. Yet most players waste more shots here than anywhere else on the course. A 3 putt is damaging to your confidence as well as your score – usually it's the result of a poor first putt. It's vital to work on a repeat-

PUTT TO A LARGER TARGET
When faced with a long putt try to roll your ball into an imaginary 3-4ft (1-1.5m) circle around the hole. Don't attempt to sink the shot. By setting an easier target you stand more chance of getting the ball close to the pin – expecting to hole it increases the pressure on you. If you try to sink a long putt you focus your attention on the hole rather than the stroke needed to combat the speed and slopes of the green. Widening the target is a psychological trick that works.

THE PENDULUM ACTION

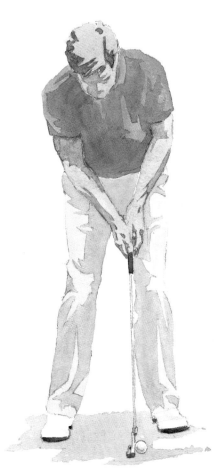

1 BALL OPPOSITE INSIDE OF LEFT HEEL
Stand with the ball opposite the inside of your left heel and your left eye directly over the ball. Your address position must be relaxed. Use the reverse overlap grip to help your feel for the shot.

2 SQUARE CLUBFACE
Keep the sole of the clubhead close to the ground for the first 12in (30cm) of the takeaway. To create the pendulum action of hands, arms and shoulders, keep the clubface and the back of your left hand square to the line of the putt for as long as possible on the backswing.

Late strike for smooth roll
For an even roll, place the ball opposite the inside of your left heel. Impact occurs late – on the upstroke – with the clubhead smoothly striking the ball forward.

If the ball is central in your stance impact is at the lowest point of the stroke. The clubhead hits down on the ball, pressing it slightly into the ground and causing it to bobble off line.

able putting stroke so that you can putt well from long distances.

Putting is the one area of the game where the high handicapper can perform as well as the low handicapper. This is because the stroke doesn't rely on power or an athletic swing. You can even practise putting in your own home.

Long putts are precision strokes. You must develop feel, intense concentration and an ability to read the green correctly.

ROLL THE BALL CLOSE

Although many players try to sink every putt – whatever the distance from the hole – they fail to hole most putts over 20ft (6m). This is true of even the most legendary players.

From beyond this distance you should try to stop your ball within 3ft (1m) of the hole. Don't expect

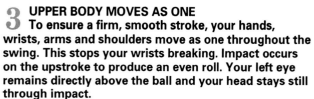

3 **UPPER BODY MOVES AS ONE**
To ensure a firm, smooth stroke, your hands, wrists, arms and shoulders move as one throughout the swing. This stops your wrists breaking. Impact occurs on the upstroke to produce an even roll. Your left eye remains directly above the ball and your head stays still through impact.

4 **KEEP YOUR HEAD STILL**
Even as the clubhead lifts up on the followthrough the clubface stays square to the line of the putt. As you complete the stroke – and not before – your head turns to face the hole. Your backswing and followthrough should be of equal length.

to sink it – if you hole a long putt accept it as a bonus. When you're a lengthy distance from the hole it's more important that you don't take 3 to get down.

READING THE GREEN

To assess your stroke accurately you must analyse two factors – the speed of the green and the lie of the land. Never be complacent – no two greens are the same.

Green speeds vary from course to course, season to season and at times even hole to hole. This happens for many reasons – mainly the soil type, its drainage and the type and length of the grass. The weather conditions are also important.

Bear in mind that the faster the green the more precisely you need to judge the speed and line of a putt, as the ball breaks more acutely on fast greens.

You must also assess the lie of the land between your ball and the hole. The slope of the green affects the line of the putt. Will the ball travel straight or curve left to right?

SPEED AND LINE

The steeper the slope the greater the curve and further left or right of the hole you must aim.

To putt well, both speed and slope must be judged correctly. Checking for slopes is fairly obvious to the eye, but speed is a mixture of experience and trial and error. Most 3 putts are caused by misjudging the pace. Try to get a feel for pace early in your round and learn from it.

For longer putts, assessing speed is more important than gauging the line as distance from the hole gets bigger. This is because there is less margin for error over long

distances.

You should not be more than 3ft (1m) off line from wherever you putt. A slight miscalculation in pace can result in your ball finishing 10-12ft (3-4m) away. Some greens are so fast that even the smallest boost in putter head speed means a difference of 10-15 ft (3-5m).

To become an accurate long putter you must combine correct green reading with a repeatable stroke.

REVERSE OVERLAP GRIP

Remember that the putting grip is similar to the standard overlapping grip – with one small difference. The forefinger of your left hand rests along two fingers of your right hand. This reverse overlap grip gives you greater feel and reduces the chances of left wrist break.

MOVE AS ONE

1 BACKSWING
Hold a club lengthways between your chest and upper arms before adopting your putting stance and starting your backswing.

Take an open stance – it helps you to see the line – and make sure your hands are square to the line of the putt. The ball should be opposite the inside of your left heel. This is slightly further forward in your stance than normal.

2 IMPACT
The club under your arms forces your shoulders, hands and arms to move as one unit through impact – if they don't, you drop the club.

Impact occurs later than usual – on the upstroke – to help produce a smooth, even roll.

Stand with your left eye over the ball. This lets you look directly along the line of the putt. If it feels uncomfortable, your putter must

3 THROUGHSWING
Your hands are still passive as your upper body – which moves as one unit throughout – completes the throughswing.

be either too long or too short for your height and needs changing.

Aim the clubface square to the line of the putt. Take the club a way with both hands – everything must work together – keeping the back of your left hand and the clubface square to the line of the putt. Keep the sole of the clubhead close to the ground, without letting it touch.

PENDULUM ACTION

Imagine the clubhead as a pendulum – moving back and through impact on the same line. Your hands should be passive – let your hands, wrists, arms and shoulders move as one to create a smooth, unhurried stroke.

The length of the putt determines how far back you take the clubhead. The backswing and throughswing should be the same length. This promotes even clubhead speed as you swing through. Don't speed up or slow down the club through impact – it affects the putt's pace.

Practise your putting regularly to develop a consistent technique and a feel for the shot.

Play it with a sand wedge
To get the feel of striking the ball on the upstroke, practise putting with a sand wedge. With the ball opposite the inside of your left heel, try to strike so that the leading clubface edge makes contact with the middle of the ball.

Unless impact is perfect, the ball jumps and bobbles towards the hole. Only when the roll is smooth and even is your putting stroke correct. Don't practise this on the course – you should not take divots on the green.

Sloping putts

Approaching a sloping putt well briefed and in the right frame of mind is the best way to hole it.

Many simple-looking holes are strengthened by heavily contoured greens, so make life easier for yourself by taking precautions.

ASSESS THE GREEN

Many parkland courses have relatively flat greens – you can deal with these fairly easily if you have a smooth putting stroke.

Heathland and links courses are

a more complicated matter – their greens are designed to make you concentrate until your ball disappears into the hole.

When top players practise before a tournament, they size up the green from all angles. Putting from every part of the green helps them learn the best spot on which to land their approach shots – if they're on target they can look forward to a birdie putt.

You can make putting on sloping greens a lot easier by copying the pros. If you play the same course

regularly, make a note of the best and worst parts of the greens. Aim your approach shots to the areas which offer the straightest putts.

Don't be content to hit the green anywhere – the most inviting spot may leave a three-putt.

GREEN SPEED

To assess how much the ball will move on a slope, you must get a feeling for the speed of the green. If the speed of the practice green

USE THE PIN
Play a sloping putt smoothly and confidently. Have the flag attended if it helps you gauge the slopes – though the pin must be removed after you've hit the ball.

Shade your eyes
To concentrate on the line of your putt, crouch down on your haunches and shade your eyes as you read the green. This helps give you a clearer, better defined picture of the putt you have to make than a wide and distracting view of the whole green – which disturbs your concentration.

PUTTING ACROSS A SIDESLOPE

READ THE PUTT
After you've read your putt play a smooth, straight shot along your imaginary ball-to-target line.

SPEED AND LINE
Some sloping putts have a huge borrow. Both speed and line have to be spot on if you're to get the ball close.

LET IT ROLL DOWN
Your ball-to-target line should account for the slope, so that a straight putt along your chosen path rolls down to the hole of its own accord.

is the same as the greens on the course where you play, spend some time putting beforehand. You'll putt far more confidently during your round.

The speed of your putt affects its line. A softly struck putt reacts to the subtle slopes more acutely than a firmly hit shot. If the green is fast, hit softly so that you don't overhit – allow for movement.

Bear in mind that a putt will not swing as far on a wet green as it does on dry grass. A putt on a wet green may leave a track in the grass as well, which gives an excellent indication of the swing.

Look at your putt from all angles to check the line – one view on its own could deceive.

Whatever the slope on your line, hit your putts straight. Let the borrow you've allowed roll your ball towards the hole. Never try to curve or spin a putt. Keep a positive image of the line in your mind and hit smoothly.

Uphill and downhill putts

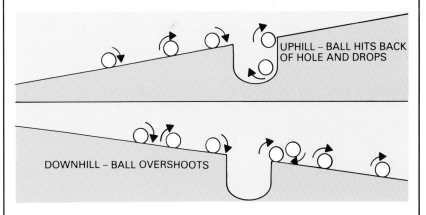

UPHILL – BALL HITS BACK OF HOLE AND DROPS

DOWNHILL – BALL OVERSHOOTS

Always try to give yourself an uphill putt rather than a downhill one. A fast uphill putt that hits the back of the hole may still drop in. But a speedy downhill putt is risky – even if it's dead on line the momentum may send your ball flying over the hole and off into the distance.

Charge or die putting

To achieve a consistent putting game on sloping greens, it is important to know when to attack and when to defend. A firmly struck, aggressive putt aimed at the back of the hole is called a charge. For a die putt you need a more calculating, cautious approach – the aim being to roll the ball gently up to the hole so it just topples into the cup.

Your technique for hitting either a charge or die putt remains exactly the same as normal. The difference between the shots is how firmly the putt is struck and the line taken. Across a slope, a charge putt travels to the hole along a straighter path than a die, which is given a wider berth.

As you hit the charge putt fairly straight, you must also strike the ball firmly to counter the effect of the slope. You have to hit a die putt on a wider line because it needs a softer strike, so the slope has more time to affect the ball's path.

AGGRESSION OR DEFENCE

The perfect time to hit a charge putt is on an uphill slope – even if the ball breaks. Coming down the green across the same slope, hit a die putt to limit the risk of the ball racing past the hole if you miss.

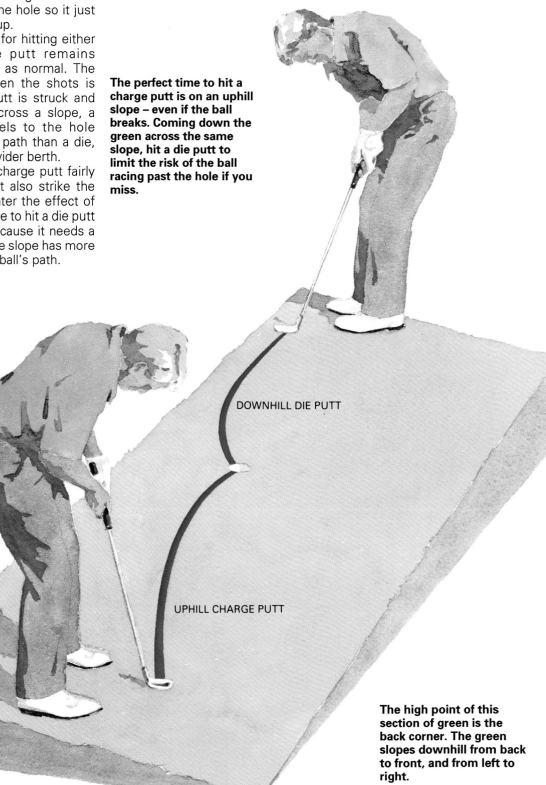

DOWNHILL DIE PUTT

UPHILL CHARGE PUTT

The high point of this section of green is the back corner. The green slopes downhill from back to front, and from left to right.

SPEED AND LINE

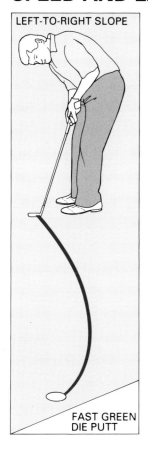

LEFT-TO-RIGHT SLOPE

FAST GREEN
DIE PUTT

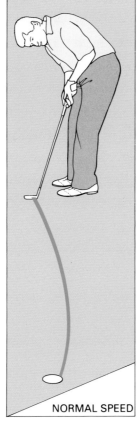

NORMAL SPEED

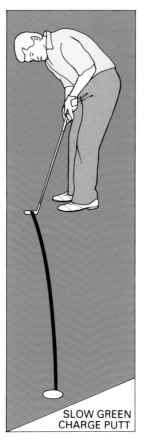

SLOW GREEN
CHARGE PUTT

SLICK GREEN
When a green has been newly mown for a competition it's usually very fast. You should give the ball more width and try to die the ball into the hole, reducing the risk of three putting.

MEDIUM PACED
On the same-sloped green of normal speed your decision to charge or die depends on how confident you feel, and whether you need to attack or defend your score. It's foolish to charge if a two putt wins you the hole.

SLOW AND GRASSY
When the same green hasn't been cut for a few days and is slow, the ball doesn't break as much as normal so you can afford to charge most of your putts. Even if you miss, the ball shouldn't run too far by.

masterclass

Palmer's charging
In his heyday one of the great trademarks of Arnold Palmer's game was the way he used to attack the hole with his putts. He was never afraid of aiming for the back of the hole and giving the ball a good rap. Even if he missed, he was such a fine putter that the return was always holeable. The famous Palmer charging putts helped him win seven major titles.

DO OR DIE

The decision whether to play a charge or die comes with experience. Think about the slope, the state of play and the speed of the green.

Slope: Any uphill putt is a potential charge. You can afford to be bold with the shot if you know that – should you miss – the ball would not go too far past. But there is little point in charging a downhill putt, because if you miss the ball rolls well past the hole. One downhill exception is when the green is so slow that the ball can't go too far past the hole.

Hit the die instead of the charge if you have to putt across a very steep slope. A charge gathers pace on the slope and unless you hole out the ball runs by.

State of play: You can take an aggressive approach to a downhill putt if you need a birdie to avoid losing a hole or the match. But there is no point in hitting a charge when you have the luxury of two putts to win a hole or competition, even if it's uphill. Be content to take the two putts by dying the ball at the hole.

Speed: When a green is lightning fast you should aim to die the ball at the hole. On a very slow green you can charge most putts unless it's severely downhill.

PACE AND PRACTICE

Whatever your choice, judging the pace of the putt is all important. Knowing how firmly to hit a putt along different lines comes with experience. You should experiment on the practice putting green.

For both types of putt you must pick a spot to aim at. With a die putt it's best to pinpoint a spot you want the ball to roll over between you and the hole. With a charge, choose a point level with the hole and aim to hit the ball at it. If you read the break properly the ball hits the back of the hole and drops in.

When you're deciding how hard and how wide you need to hit the ball towards the hole, it's essential to visualize the path and how the slope affects it.

Being able to weigh up the facts quickly and make the right decision on the putting green – do you want to charge or die? – is vital to protect your score. Often it's a decision that must be made under pressure in a match – prepare yourself by brushing up these putting skills.

Putting on two tiers

When your approach shot lands on one tier and the flag is on the other, you should still need no more than two putts. Learning to putt well on a two-tier green saves precious strokes.

Although the putting technique is the same as on a flat green, judging the bank is the key to playing well. Understanding how a ball behaves when it rolls over the step is half the battle.

Going straight up or down the bank is purely a matter of judging how hard to hit the ball. But when you're faced with a putt across the green and over the bank the line must be taken into account.

CHANGING PATHS

The path of the ball changes twice on its way to the hole. It first alters when the ball runs on to the bank between the tiers, and changes again when the putt reaches the other tier. The final path is parallel to the initial line.

For example, if you need to putt

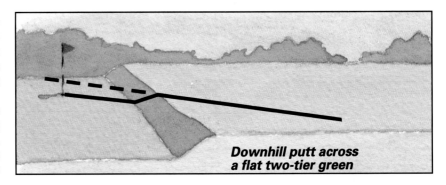

Downhill putt across a flat two-tier green

Uphill putt across a sloping two-tier green

TWO PUTT ZONE

WEAK PUTT

AVOID THREE PUTTING
Putting on split level greens needs careful thought to calculate the pace and line of the ball.

For a **downhill putt** going across a flat two-tier green from left to right you must aim to the right of the hole. The bank turns the ball left but it straightens out towards the hole on reaching the lower tier. The path the ball takes on the lower tier is parallel to the initial line if you judge the pace correctly.

When going **up the bank** aim to hit the ball into an imaginary two putt zone around the hole. Remember to take into account the cross slope on the top tier.

You must always get the ball on to the top tier with your first putt, even if it goes past the hole. Never hit the ball too weakly so it rolls back down the slope – a three putt is almost a certainty.

up and across – from left to right – a two-tier green, you must aim at a point wide and left of the hole. The ball moves to the right on the bank then straightens again when it reaches the top tier.

The amount the ball breaks depends on how high and steep the bank is, and the pace of the putt. The higher the bank, the

more the ball moves off line, and the wider of the hole you must aim. The ball is less affected by the bank if it's rolling fast. If the green also slopes across, take this into account when choosing your line.

Once you have chosen your line you must judge the pace.

If you're **going downhill** pick a

point on the edge of the bank and try to hit your ball over it. Imagine you're putting to a hole on the step. The strength of the putt should be just enough for the ball to trickle over.

Make sure the ball reaches the lower tier every time – a ball 10ft (3m) past the hole is better than leaving it on the top tier. If the hole is a long way from the foot of the bank, aim at a point on the bottom tier to make certain the ball reaches the target.

When **putting uphill** on to the top tier, choose a spot past the hole to counter the effect of the bank. Imagine you're playing to a hole beyond the actual flag. If you judge the pace correctly and take the proper line the ball should finish fairly close to the pin. You can lag your first putt to give an easy second.

Judgement putting
When faced with a putt on a two-tier green you must make sure that you two putt – with practice it isn't that difficult. Fix your mind on avoiding the three putt – regard holing your first putt as a bonus.

To calculate the pace and line

coming across the green and down a bank you must understand how the step and any slope affect the ball. Aim slightly right of the flag – visualize putting to an imaginary target at the top of the bank. The ball is carried away naturally by the bank towards the hole.

DOWN AND ACROSS TWO-TIER GREEN

IMAGINARY TARGET

masterclass

Canny Canizares
In the 1989 Ryder Cup match, José-Maria Canizares had two putts from 55ft (17m) on the 18th to retain the trophy for Europe. But he had to come downhill over a bank – judgement was all important.

He stroked the putt perfectly so it just rolled to the edge of the bank and then trickled down to within 3ft (1m) of the hole. He holed the next to beat Ken Green and secure the tie.

Steep slope putting

Judging pace is critical if you are to avoid three putting on steeply sloping greens. But a fine judgement of speed must be linked with good reading of the line. The pace determines the line. You must first gauge the weight of the putt, then concentrate on the line and balance the two considerations.

DIFFERING APPROACHES

Aim to hole your first putt only when it's close to the pin. From long range think of two putting, as three putts are always a danger and holing out must be seen as a bonus.

Straight uphill: This is easily the simplest putt on a steeply sloping green. You can afford to hit the ball firmly and it still should drop because of the angle of the hole.

But be wary of overhitting the ball on a long putt – you could leave yourself a very awkward downhill putt.

From short range, make a smooth stroke and hit the ball firmly at the back of the hole.

Straight downhill: The pace is all important. Any putt going at even slightly more than perfect speed has little chance of dropping.

To help you judge the pace from long range, pick a point – perhaps an old hole or small mark on the green – between you and the hole. Choose a spot just a few inches away on a very steep green. Then play a normal putt to your spot – the slope carries the ball the rest of the way.

Always make sure you hit the ball with enough pace to send it past the hole should you miss. A

putt from 6ft (2m) straight back up the hill is far better than facing a tricky downhiller of 3ft (1m).

From short range concentrate on the line. Take time to set the blade exactly square to the target line because a downhill putt that catches the lip spins out unless going very slowly. Never leave a putt short from close range – it's a waste of a stroke.

Long putt across the slope: The ideal putt across a steep green is for the ball to topple in from the

EXPLORE ALL ANGLES
There is an art to balancing the line and pace on a steeply sloping green – an understanding of how the ball behaves from all angles makes putting much easier. From long range aim to knock your ball just past the hole to leave an uphill second. Holing out is a bonus.

top side. For this you judge the weight of the shot so the ball comes almost to a standstill above but nearly level with the hole. The ball then rolls down the slope and comes in from almost 90°.

But be realistic – aim to two putt on most occasions. Your main thought should be to lag the ball and regard holing out first time as a bonus.

Pace and line are vital. If you under or overhit the ball – even if you've chosen a good line – you're left with the same awkward type of putt but from a slightly shorter distance. Hit the ball too low and it gathers speed down the slope and runs well by. Hit too high and

the ball stays up on the top side and you're left with a tricky down-hill breaking putt.

Short putt across the slope: Aim at a point level with the hole. Again almost stop the ball on the top side so that it rolls slowly down towards the hole.

Always allow more break than you think – it's better to be on the top side (known as the pro side) because the ball has a chance of dropping-in as it trickles slowly down the hill. Once the ball falls below the line of the hole it can't break back up the hill.

Die the ball into the hole rather than play an aggressive stroke. This eliminates any risk of the putt

lipping out and running away down the slope.

Combination putt: When you're faced with a putt across the slope, but also either up or down the green, there is one vital point to bear in mind. The slower the ball is travelling the more it breaks.

A downhill putt across a slope needs to be given a much wider berth than an uphill putt with the same amount of break.

A downhiller has to played with caution – unless it's definitely holeable be content to two putt. An uphill putt can be hit firmly on a narrow line – the ball breaks near the hole, and you can afford to be aggressive.

pro tip

Toe tip
An excellent way to gain more control over a downhill putt is to hit the ball off the toe of the putter. This deadens the strike – the ball doesn't come off the clubface as fast as it would if struck in the middle of the blade.

It's especially useful when you need just to set the ball rolling on a very steep slope or down lightning fast greens.

Pace pointer
If you find difficulty in judging the pace of a downhill putt – particularly with break – hit a normal putt at a chosen point between you and the hole. It may be an old hole, a small leaf or patch on the green.

If you have judged the slope properly the ball is carried past this point and breaks naturally down towards the hole. The faster the putt the nearer your imaginary point should be.

This method helps you focus on your putting stroke rather than worrying about the putt itself.

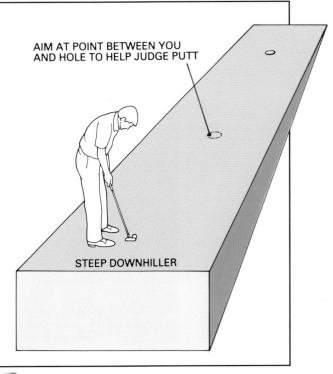

AIM AT POINT BETWEEN YOU AND HOLE TO HELP JUDGE PUTT

STEEP DOWNHILLER

masterclass

The Crenshaw touch
Ben Crenshaw is regarded by his fellow pros as one of the greatest putters of modern times. He combines a rock solid stroke with his natural ability to read greens. The American's understanding of how a steeply sloping green affects putts has helped him gain this reputation.

Crenshaw accurately judges the pace and line of even the fastest and most steeply sloping greens. His touch was at its best when he conquered the world's hardest greens at Augusta and won the 1984 Masters.

PRACTICE MAKES PERFECT

To help you improve your stroke you will need to perform specific putting exercises. There are various fun ways to practise which will prevent you from becoming bored; boredom is the excuse players often use for not going to the putting green. Set yourself achievable goals, work for half an hour on a regular basis and just watch your technique improve.

Ian Woosnam's caddie Phil Morbey helps him line up a putt at the Suntory World Matchplay Final in 1987. Morbey's advice during the tournament helped Woosnam win.

Plumb-bobbing

Greens are full of deceptive slopes and undulations, which make your putt more difficult. Plumb-bobbing is an effective way of measuring the slope of a green and is used by many top professionals to gauge the line of their putts.

The vertical line created by hanging the putter in front of you gives a useful pointer for the subtle slopes around you on the green. On hilly courses it helps you keep an idea of the true horizontal, as the humps and hollows can deceive.

ASSESS THE BREAK

You can also plumb-bob to assess the amount of break in your putt. Sometimes a putt can look straight but be affected by slopes that you can't see with the naked eye. Plumb-bobbing helps you to adjust your putt accordingly.

To plumb-bob correctly, you need to use your master eye. To find out which is your master eye, hold your forefinger at arm's length and look at it, aiming at a point in the background. Then look with each eye separately, closing the other as you do so. The eye which shows your finger nearest to the point in the background you're aiming at is your master eye.

Stand a few paces behind your

HOW DOES YOUR PUTT BREAK? Sometimes it's difficult to see the break of your putt with the naked eye. The technique known as plumb-bobbing gives a vertical reference to help you gain an idea of the correct borrow.

ball, on a direct line with the hole. Take hold of your putter with one hand and hold it at arm's length, opposite your master eye. The putter must hang straight in relation to your viewpoint. Make sure that the toe of your clubhead points directly towards or away from you.

Line up the centre of your ball with the lower part of the shaft. Let your master eye come up the shaft until it is level with the hole. If there is a slope, the hole will be to the right or left of the shaft – adjust your borrow accordingly. If the slope is obvious, plumb-bob to confirm exactly how much.

Check the cut of the hole

Sometimes the last few rolls before the ball reaches the hole can have a marked effect on your putt. After plumb-bobbing, check how the hole is cut.
Greenkeepers often pull up the hole cutter at an angle. This means that one side of the hole is higher than the other. For instance, if plumb-bobbing has shown you have a left-to-right putt, and the hole is cut higher to the right, you must adjust the line – the putt is now almost straight.

PLUMB-BOBBING TECHNIQUE

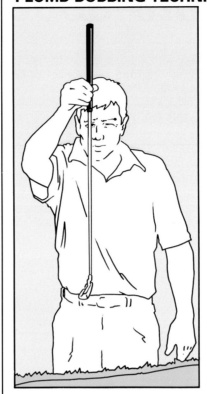
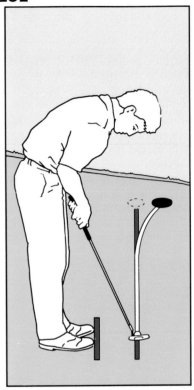

Let the club hang naturally. Make sure the toe of the putter is pointing either precisely towards or away from you so that it hangs vertical to your viewpoint. With the shaft lined up with the centre of the ball, raise your master eye until it is level with the hole. If the hole is on the right of the shaft, aim left to allow for the borrow – and vice versa.

masterclass

Strange plumb-bobbing

In 1989, Curtis Strange became the first player since Ben Hogan in 1951 to defend the US Open title successfully. As hearts were sinking elsewhere, Strange's use of plumb-bobbing gave him the confidence to go for putts. His final round over the tough Oak Hill course contained 16 pars – in part thanks to his smooth and positive putting stroke.

Judging the grain

Although reading the green correctly is essential, you can hole even more putts by judging the grain properly.

The grain is the direction in which the grass grows. In the mild climates of the British Isles and northern Europe, grass grows straight up, so the grain hardly affects your putt. However, the grass is mown up and down, pushing it in one direction and then the other. These stripes give the same effect as natural grain.

EFFECTS OF GRAIN
The same putt varies according to the grain (the direction in which the grass grows or is mown). In warm climates, the natural grain can slow down, speed up or curve a putt. Mowing the grass can have a similar effect in colder climates.

WITH THE GRAIN
If the grass is pale, you are putting with the grain, and your ball travels quickly.

AGAINST THE GRAIN
The same putt hit against the grain runs more slowly and falls short of the hole.

ACROSS THE GRAIN
As the putt meets the join it is almost like hitting a wall. The ball veers as a result.

ACROSS THE GRAIN
The putt curves away as it strikes the join, along the left-to-right line of the mini 'wall'.

A green with a strong grain looks dull and dark when you stand on one side, and shiny and light from the other. When it looks light and shiny, you are putting with the grain, and the ball runs very quickly. With the green looking dull and dark, a putt is against the grain and runs relatively slowly.

In warmer countries, such as Australia, South Africa and the holiday areas of southern Europe, the natural grain is pronounced. Recognizing it and understanding what it does to the ball's path is as important as gauging the slope and line of your putt.

READING THE GRAIN

Golf courses in hot countries usually have greens laid with either Bermuda or bent grass. These are grasses which shoot up quickly in the sun and also grow in specific directions.

The direction the grass grows depends on where the green is – if there is sea or a natural lake nearby, it's very likely that the grain leads towards it.

Alternatively, the grain may point where the prevailing wind is heading, or it could lead away from mountains. Taking all these factors into account is vital if you are putting on grainy greens.

SLOPE AND GRAIN

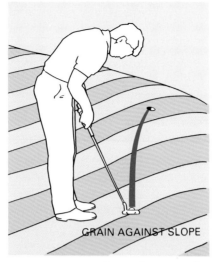

GRAIN AGAINST SLOPE

GRAIN WITH SLOPE

When the green slopes downwards and the grain runs against the slope, the putt is almost straight. If both the slope and the grain run in the same direction, the line of your putt becomes more acute. You must allow for even more break and aim well to the left of the hole.

The same goes for the stripes left by a mower. You need to assess the grass direction before you can judge the pace of your putt correctly. The ball has to roll over the join between each stripe, so you also have to allow for this making your putt break.

An uphill putt against the grain is extra slow. But the same putt with the grain may counteract the effect of the slope, and make a normal – or fast – stroke.

If the grain runs sideways across the line of your putt, it has the same effect as a sideslope. This means curving the putt with the grain.

If you have a left-to-right putt, and the grain runs in the same direction, the break becomes even more acute. When the line of your putt goes against the grain, its break is almost cancelled.

Ben Crenshaw: master putter
Ben Crenshaw is widely regarded as the most successful putter in modern golf. He is living proof of the old golf saying, 'Drive for show, putt for dough.'

On occasions, when Crenshaw's erratic swing isn't working too reliably, he stays in contention in many tournaments because of his beautifully tuned putting stroke.

Crenshaw putts so well because he perfected the firm-wristed pendulum action. He is also a superb green reader. Knowing that the slightest misjudgment can make a putt lip out, he studies the green and the grain from all angles until he is sure of his pace and line.

The confidence that comes from assessing the grain and slopes accurately is essential to playing a positive stroke.

Dry or damp?
A hot sun dries out the grass very quickly. If the green is sunken, or has trees overhanging it, parts of it may remain in shadow for longer than others. This means that sections of the same green can be either bone dry or damp.

Remember this when you assess your putt – damp grass can slow the ball down considerably, while dryness means a fast putt and a more acute break.

Holing six-footers

Being able to hole out consistently from the awkward range of about 6ft (1.8m) is vital for good scoring. It's a confidence booster to know that even if you miss the green and your chip finishes that tricky distance away you have a very good chance of saving par.

Problems with this shot are mainly mental – a negative attitude can hinder your technique. The length of swing is so short that it's hard for a proper technique to go drastically wrong on its own.

STRAIGHT BACK

Although the club naturally moves inside the line on the backswing of a long putt, the path should be almost straight back along the ball-to-target line on a short putt. There is only a very slight move inside – if at all – on a six footer.

The crucial points are at impact and the followthrough. The blade should always return square at impact, and you must follow through along the ball-to-target line on a straight putt. This reduces the risk of pushing or pulling the

ball and missing the putt.

If you swing a putter along the target line on a straight putt, only the pace or a bad kick can keep the ball out. Your stance should be sturdy but relaxed, and your action free of tension and smooth

CONFIDENCE AND TECHNIQUE
Six footers are awkward. While you expect to hole a short putt, and finding the cup from afar is a bonus, holing out from about a flag's length away is puttable – just. Be bold – all you need is confidence and a sound technique.

SIX FOOTER SUCCESS

1 TARGET LINE TAKEAWAY
Your takeaway must be smooth with no wrist break – you should be conscious of the club moving back along the ball-to-target line. The clubhead moves naturally inside on the backswing (below), but the movement should be only very slight.

2 DOWN THE LINE
The blade must be square at impact. Make sure the club follows through along the target line – it mustn't move to the inside. The proper line keeps the clubface square to the target for as long as possible, reducing the risk of a pull or a push.

3 CONTROLLED FINISH
Hold the club at the finish position. Resist the tendency to jerk the putter back to the address position after impact – this leads to a jabbing stroke. Notice how the head has remained still throughout the stroke. Don't look up until you hear the putt drop, or your body can turn at impact and pull the ball off line.

yet controlled. Keep your grip light, and make sure you never break your wrists.

Stay perfectly still throughout the stroke. To help you achieve this, never look up to watch the ball rolling towards the hole. Wait until you hear the putt drop. This helps keep the putter swinging on the proper path.

On a breaking putt the technique remains the same but you must now judge the line and pace carefully. Don't be tempted to guide the ball at the hole – once you have chosen your line, putt straight along it letting the slope – not your putter blade – turn the ball back towards the target.

Confidence is the key – build it up by going out to practice. A positive attitude helps you relax and make a good stroke when it matters. Having negative thoughts on the greens can destroy even the best putting technique. Always try to be positive and assume you're going to hole out every six footer.

pro tip

Eye drops
It is a great help to be able to turn your head while standing over a putt to see straight down the line to the hole. For this your eyes should be directly over the ball. To find the position, hold a ball on the bridge of your nose and then drop it. Where the ball lands is where you should place it in your stance.

EYES OVER BALL

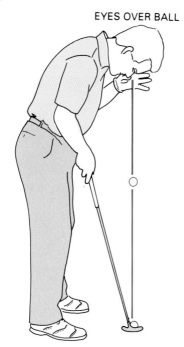

pro tip

Tee peg training

Placing two sets of tee pegs in the practice green to channel your club is an excellent way to ingrain the proper stroke into your game. The sets should be about 10in (25cm) apart, and just wide enough for your clubhead to pass through.

Place a ball in the middle of the rectangle formed by the tees. Swing the putter away and through the back two pegs without touching either one. Hitting a peg means you have taken the club away on the wrong line.

Swing through smoothly making sure the putter blade travels between the front tees. This ensures the blade follows through along the target line.

Hold the finish position. Notice how a straight line can be drawn from the centre of the rectangle through clubhead, ball and to the hole.

masterclass

Fearless Faldo

Double Open champion Nick Faldo is cool under pressure and expects to hole six footers. Because his technique is excellent – straight back and through – and his temperament ideal, the awkward length putt holds no fear for him. With an extremely smooth and confident stroke he misses very few putts of a flag's length.

Faldo's stroke held up under the severest of pressure from about 5ft (1.5m) in the final round of the 1987 Open at Muirfield. He had to hole out several times from this tricky length to save his par. Incredibly, the man from Hertfordshire parred all 18 holes – at the last, this missable one clinched the title.

Green drills

Putting practice is vital, but still there isn't as much time spent on it as there should be. What can put people off is the boredom of hitting stroke after stroke at a hole.

You need to make putting practice enjoyable while improving your touch naturally. Using various drills and games helps you to become a better judge of line and weight, and to groove your stroke without unnecessary toil and boredom.

Many useful drills don't involve a hole at all, and some need more than one person to be any use. Try to find the ones that you enjoy most, but also those that work on the worst aspects of your putting game – perhaps judgment of distance.

It's important to develop all facets of your putting game so you're solid from both short and long range – not just in a friendly but when the heat is on and the pressure of competition is fierce.

MEASURED WEIGHT
To find your feel for distance it's best not to aim at a hole – it can be distracting. To gauge long range putts, simply press a tee peg into the practice green and try to lay every putt dead – within 2ft (60cm). Playing with a couple of friends helps as well – score a point every time you knock your ball closest to the tee. Perhaps even play for a small wager to help you cope with pressure.

To develop a touch for medium range putts lay out three tee pegs in a line, the first about 15ft (4.5m) away and then at 10ft (3m) intervals. Hit two balls at each peg and keep repeating the exercise. This teaches you to take a putt on individually and judge the pace each time, which helps your touch.

▶ BOWLING GREEN

One of the most enjoyable ways to hone your judgment of pace and line is to play bowls. You need two or more players, three balls each and a jack – the target ball. Player 1 knocks the jack down the green, then hits his first ball towards it trying to go as close as possible. Player 2 then has a go to beat his rival. Take alternate shots until you have hit all the balls.

To score, judge whose ball is closest. If you have the nearest ball award yourself a point. If two balls are closer than your rival's nearest, award two points. And if you are lucky enough to have knocked three inside your opponent's, claim three points. Play until one of you has reached 21.

Allen's drill

US pro Michael Allen uses a very simple but effective practice aid to groove his putting stroke. He lays two clubs down parallel to each other – at just over putter head width apart – and aligns them at the hole, so that if he hits a straight putt the ball drops.

This means he has to take the putter back on a straight line or else it collides with the clubs on the ground. But he must also keep the blade square to target back and through the ball if the putt is to drop.

Allen's hard work on his putting finally paid dividends in 1989 when he won the Scottish Open. Five strokes back with one round to play he shot an amazing 63 to pip Ian Woosnam and José-Maria Olazabal. With 7 birdies and an eagle in the last 13 holes he needed only 22 putts.

He ended the year tied for 9th in the putting statistics – averaging under 30 putts per round – and carried this form to the US Qualifying School where he earned his card for 1990.

▼ ALL IN A ROW

Although trying to hole out every time isn't always a good idea – because you can easily become bored and lose your confidence – one drill works well on the short putts. Line five or six balls up on a flat piece of green about 12in (30cm) apart, starting from 3ft (1m) out.

Attempt to hole the first ball. If you do, move on to the next, and so on until you fail to hole out. When you fail, retrieve all the balls and start again. The object of the exercise is hole out every ball one after the other. This drill helps your short putt stroke and does wonders for your concentration and determination. It makes you really want to hole out each time as you know you must start all over again if one fails to drop.

pro tip

Sweeten your touch

WEIGHTING GAME
To ensure accurately weighted putts, it's critical to cultivate your touch and feel from medium and long range. Your muscles rely on being sent a precise message from your brain about how hard to hit the putt.

To help you ingrain a sense of distance and weight into your game, forget about the line of your putts for a moment. Go on to the practice green with about ten balls and position yourself 15ft to 40ft (4.5-12m) away from the edge. Then putt each ball towards the fringe – playing to a hole distracts your gauging of weight as you have to think about the line of the putt as well. Try to stop the ball as close as possible to the edge of the green without ever running up on to the fringe.

Play against someone else to make it more interesting – perhaps for a little wager – and score a point every time you knock one closest to the edge.

The action of putting to a band rather than a hole naturally helps your perception and feel for length. This drill should give you confidence to judge long range putts out on the course and avoid the dreaded 3 putt.

BLIND MAN'S PUTT

Putting without ever looking up to see where the ball has gone is a remarkably tell-tale drill. It gives you an accurate indication of your natural feel for weight.

With roughly ten balls, aim to a hole-free area. Take one ball at a time and try to stroke it to a point about 25ft (7.5m) away. Don't look up between shots, just roll the next ball towards you and repeat your stroke. Try to keep everything the same – the line, rhythm and strength. The idea is to finish up with the balls as tightly grouped as possible.

Only after the last ball is on it's way may you look up. With putts of that length you should be able to throw an imaginary ring – about 2 ft (75cm) in diameter – around all the balls. Keep practising until you succeed, then move on to a longer distance. For every 5ft (1.5m) you add to the length of the putt, the diameter of your target area should increase by 6in (15cm).

This drill is better than the usual blindfold exercise – putting with your eyes shut – since you can still concentrate on your stroke, and your ball striking is more consistent. Both your touch and putting stroke improve together.

Short putt slip-ups

Failing to hole short putts is not only annoying but is damaging to your scorecard. It can be a mental problem, but is just as likely to be caused by a slight fault in your putting stroke.

Q I struggle to hole short, breaking putts – I tend to pull a right to lefter, and push the one from left to right. And even my straight putts are erratic in a strong wind. Can you help?

A The most common cause of missing short, breaking putts is if you guide the ball at the hole. Even if you aim your blade right of the hole for a right-to-left breaker, the natural tendency is to close the blade slightly into impact in an attempt to hit the ball directly at the hole. A pulled putt to the left is the result.

You don't mean to, but it is something built into the brain that tells you to aim straight at the hole. To avoid this mishap, you must concentrate on striking the ball at a point wide of the hole and let the slope do the work. Set up and aim the blade square to the intended path, and then stroke the ball straight towards your imaginary target. If you have judged the break and weight well, the ball should take the slope and drop in.

The problem with putting in a strong wind is that you can be blown off balance easily. And because a short putt stroke is such a small and precise swing, the tiniest body movement can ruin your action. Two adjustments help your balance and short putt technique in a wind. Adopt a wider stance than normal to give yourself extra stability, and grip down the putter to give you more control over the clubhead.

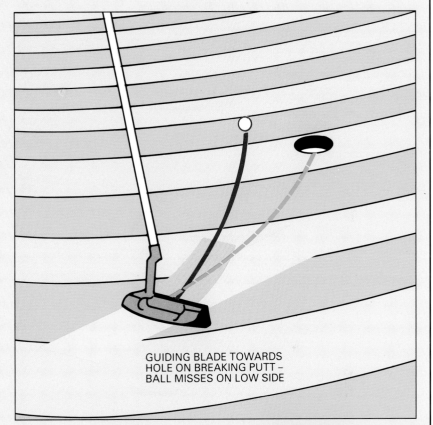

GUIDING BLADE TOWARDS HOLE ON BREAKING PUTT – BALL MISSES ON LOW SIDE

WIDER STANCE IN STRONG WIND

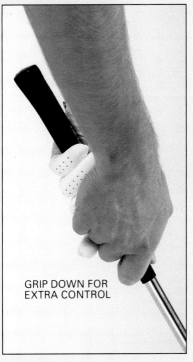

GRIP DOWN FOR EXTRA CONTROL

Q I tend to pull my short putts even if there is no break. Why?

A Your putting stroke is almost certainly incorrect. If you take the putter back slightly on the inside and then swing through impact on an in-to-in path – like a micro version of a full swing – there is only a very precise point when the blade is square.

If you're lucky the blade returns exactly square at impact. But it's also very possible that your clubface is a fraction crooked. Because you swing back to the inside you are likely to have a slightly closed blade through impact and that is why you pull your putts.

Straight back and through

To be sure of holing out from a short distance, you must have a square blade at impact. The only way you can be positive of achieving this is to swing with the blade square throughout your action.

Take the club back on a straight path along the ball-to-target line. If you now swing into and through impact along the same line while keeping your blade square, the ball rolls straight at the hole. The only way the ball won't drop is if you have misjudged the pace or something in its path knocks it off line.

PUTTER TAKEN BACK ON INSIDE LINE

PUTTER SWINGS STRAIGHT BACK ON BALL-TO-TARGET LINE

BLADE RETURNS SQUARE IF LUCKY

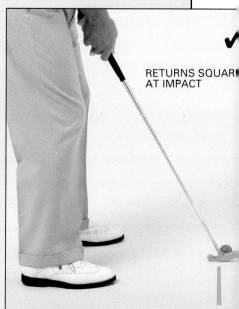

RETURNS SQUARE AT IMPACT

SWINGS TO INSIDE – LIKELY TO PULL BALL

CLUB SWINGING THROUGH ON TARGET LINE KEEPS FACE SQUARE – BALL ROLLS STRAIGHT

THE AGONY AND ECSTASY

The following pictures show the ecstasy of winning and the agony of losing. Putting is the final element of your game that you must perfect if your overall game is to improve. Whether you choose to do this sooner or later is entirely dependent on how quickly you wish to lower your handicap.

Christy O'Connor's face says it all as he misses a putt during the Dunhill Cup in 1989. The Irish team got as far as the semi-finals where O'Connor came against Tom Kite in a play-off. Ireland's hopes were dashed when Christy shot his approach to the 1st into the Swilcan Burn at St Andrews.

Left: Doug Sanders holds his breath as he watches his ball miss the hole – forcing him into a play-off with Nicklaus, his challenger for the 1970 British Open. Sanders lost. His was the shortest missed putt to win a Major until Hoch's failure in 1989.

Right: A missed putt at the 1984 Open at St Andrews helped Bernhard Langer finish second, two shots behind the winner Seve Ballesteros.

Right: David Graham registers dismay as a putt slides by during the 1981 US Masters. Despite his success on the US Tour he never seriously challenged at Augusta, although he was fifth in 1980.

Below: Ken Brown's chip to halve with the US team in the 1977 Ryder Cup missed by a couple of inches. He and his partner Mark James lost by 1 hole to Hale Irwin and Lou Graham.

Right and below: Ronan Rafferty watches expectantly then celebrates as the ball drops at the 18th at St Andrews in 1988 in his Dunhill Cup game with Australia's David Graham. It confirmed a 2-1 win, and the title for Ireland.

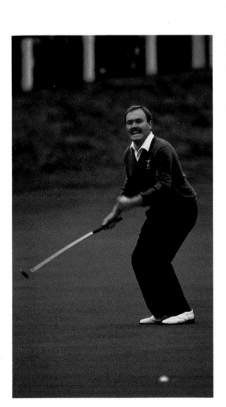

Above: Suspense is too much for Scott Hoch in the play-off with Nick Faldo at the 1989 US Masters. Nerves caused him to miss his short putt on the first extra hole.

Right: There's no doubt where this putt landed during the 1987 Ryder Cup match. Held at Muirfield Village, Ohio, the trophy went to the European team despite Kite's sound performance.